ROSENSHINE'S

Principles in Practice

By Tom Sherrington

1641 Worthington Road, Suite 210, West Palm Beach, FL 33409
717.845.6300
email: pub@learningsciences.com
learningsciences.com

Printed in the United States of America

23   22   21   20   19   1   2   3   4   5

Publisher's Cataloging-in-Publication Data
provided by Five Rainbows Cataloging Services

Names: Sherrington, Tom, author. | Cavigioli, Oliver, illustrator.
Title: Rosenshine's principles in practice / Tom Sherrington ; Oliver Cavigioli, illustrator.
Description: West Palm Beach, FL : Learning Sciences, 2019.
Identifiers: ISBN 978-1-943920-67-9 (paperback)
Subjects: LCSH: Effective teaching. | Teaching--Methodology. | Education--Research. | MESH: Medical heading. | Education--Aims and objectives. | BISAC: EDUCATION / Professional Development. | EDUCATION / Teaching Methods & Materials / General.
Classification: LCC LB1025.3 .S54 2019 (print) | LCC LB1025.3 (ebook) | DDC 371.102--dc23.

Table of Contents

ACKNOWLEDGEMENTS

I owe the existence of this book to several people. First of all, Barak Rosenshine himself for obvious reasons! I hope I've done his work justice. Then Oliver Caviglioli who drew my attention to Rosenshine's principles through his superb graphics. I'm thrilled that he found time to produce illustrations for this book alongside his many other projects. The idea for the book itself came from Mark Combes at Learning Sciences International in the US. He saw me give my Rosenshine talk at the 2018 ResearchEd event in Philadelphia organised by Eric Kalenze and felt that a short 'explainer' for teachers in the US might be useful. So this book would not exist without Mark and Eric or Tom Bennett, who has supported my involvement in ResearchEd events many times.

The UK edition has been enthusiastically embraced by Alex Sharratt at John Catt with the superb editorial oversight of Jonathan Woolgar. The US edition has been driven along by Dana Lake. I'm grateful for their support through the whole process.

I'd like to acknowledge some of the people who have helped me get to grips with the concepts in the book, directly or indirectly: Arthur Shimamura, Efrat Furst, Daniel Willingham, David Didau and Nick Rose, Paul Kirschner have helped me to develop a deeper understanding of learning processes. Finally, the staff at Oldham College and Brune Park School and my wife and Deputy Headteacher Deborah O'Connor have all helped me formulate ideas about putting theory into practice.

Why Are Barak Rosenshine's Principles of Instruction So Good?

I first encountered Barak Rosenshine's *Principles of Instruction* after the British educator and graphic illustrator Oliver Caviglioli shared his excellent visual guide on Twitter. This prompted me to seek out the *American Educator* article from 2012 where Rosenshine's ideas are set out. This article is taken almost directly from a pamphlet in The International Academy of Education (IAE) Educational Practices Series in 2010. In his pamphlet Rosenshine sets out ten research-based principles of instruction based on the ideas he and his colleagues had developed over the preceding decades.

On first reading, I was struck immediately by its brilliant clarity and simplicity, and its potential to support teachers seeking to engage with cognitive science and the wider world of education research. In the last year, Rosenshine's *Principles of Instruction* has been circulating increasingly rapidly around schools in the UK as more teachers discover its insights, sharing via social media and the growing array of grassroots teacher conferences.

The purpose of writing this short booklet is to capture some of the many discussions I've had with school leaders and teachers, taking the ideas off the page and putting them into action in the classroom. Although the principles are superbly helpful as Rosenshine has expressed them, my hope is that this booklet provides an extra layer of guidance that people find interesting and useful, informing their staff training programs or the development of their personal practice.

Four strands

The organization of ideas that make up *Principles of Instruction* has evolved over time. In *Teaching Functions* (Rosenshine & Stevens, 1986), there were six. In the IAE pamphlet, Rosenshine outlines seventeen instructional procedures that emerge from the research:

Table 1.1 Rosenshine's Seventeen Instructional Procedures

• Begin a lesson with a short review of previous learning.	• Provide models of worked-out problems.
• Present new material in small steps with student practice after each step.	• Ask students to explain what they had learned.
• Limit the amount of material students receive at one time.	• Check the responses of all students.
• Give clear and detailed instructions and explanations.	• Provide systematic feedback and corrections.
• Ask a large number of questions and check for understanding.	• Use more time to provide explanations.
• Provide a high level of active practice for all students.	• Provide many examples.
• Guide students as they begin to practice.	• Re-teach material when necessary.
	• Prepare students for independent practice.
	• Monitor students when they begin independent practice.
	• Think aloud and model steps.

From these procedures he then formulates the ten principles. In seeking to explain the principles to audiences in the UK during various ResearchEd[1] conferences, I found that it helps to condense ten ideas down to four strands. Partly this is because of the requirements of timing a conference presentation where ten ideas feels like a long list, but mainly I found that after revisiting the document many times, I was continually skipping back and forth to make these connections.

Table 1.2 The Four Strands

The Principles of Instruction	Four Strands
1. Daily Review	**Sequencing Concepts and Modeling**
2. Present new material using small steps	2. Present new material using small steps
	4. Provide Models
3. Ask questions.	8. Provide scaffolds for difficult tasks
4. Provide Models	**Questioning**
5. Guide student practice	3. Ask questions.
6. Check for student understanding.	6. Check for student understanding.
7. Obtain a high success rate.	**Reviewing Material**
8. Provide scaffolds for difficult tasks	1. Daily Review
	10. Weekly and Monthly Review
9. Independent practice.	**Stages of Practice**
10. Weekly and Monthly Review	5. Guide student practice
	7. Obtain a high success rate.
	9. Independent practice.

---

[1] ResearchEd is a UK-based organization running teacher conferences that focus on educational research and its implications for teachers and school leaders. https://researched.org.uk

I will use the four strands as the structure for this guide. But first, I'd like to explore why the *Principles of Instruction* pamphlet is receiving such an enthusiastic response and why I am so excited to adapt it for classroom use.

Bridging the research-practice divide

Rosenshine provides a highly accessible bridge between research and classroom practice. His principles are short, easy to read, and packed with insights. This is refreshing. From a teacher's perspective, research is still hard to access. A lot of original research languishes in obscure journals that most teachers don't even know exist. Even when wonderful communicators like Daniel Willingham, John Hattie, Dylan Wiliam, and, more recently, Efrat Furst, Yana Weinstein, Megan Sumeracki, and other members of The Learning Scientists[2] publish books and blogs, it is still a challenge to secure major engagement across a large group of staff in a school. This is partly due to the limitations of teachers' time – they are busy! – but it's also a matter of school culture. Schools carry a lot of inertia; teachers' habits are hard to shift. The punchy simplicity of the principles cuts through a lot of that.

In the original publication, each short section outlining one of the ten principles follows a clear and persuasive structure: **Research findings** followed by **In the classroom**. Rosenshine does a superb job of relating research findings to classroom practice in such a way that conveys the key outcome of the research without getting bogged down in methodology and problematic considerations of effect size. The 2010 paper carries all the citations for anyone wishing to look a little deeper, and they are included at

---

[2] The Learning Scientists are a group of cognitive psychological scientists interested in research in education. www.learningscientists.org

the end of this guide. There's power in the simple binary descriptor Rosenshine deploys to get his message across: **more effective** teachers vs **less effective** teachers. We all understand that implicitly there's a sliding scale—that more layers of nuance lie beneath—but 'more effective' cuts to the chase. And who doesn't want to be in that camp!?

Trustworthiness

In addition to highlighting samples of evidence, the overall tone and content of the principles give teachers confidence that these ideas are not fads; they are rooted in evidence that has stood the test of time. Rosenshine introduces his pamphlet with a brief overview of the three sources of evidence that have informed his principles:

a) Research on how our brain acquires and uses new information: *cognitive science.*
b) Research on the common classroom practices of those teachers whose students show the highest gains: *observational studies of master teachers.*
c) Findings from studies that taught learning strategies to students: *testing cognitive supports and scaffolds that help students learn complex tasks.*

He follows up with the acknowledgement that although the approaches are very different, "there is no conflict at all between the instructional suggestions that come from each of these three sources. In other words, these three sources supplement and complement each other." This fact "gives us faith in the validity of these findings."[3]

The convergence of ideas from classroom observations and cognitive science is important. If it were the case that cognitive science suggested a different set of instructional

---

[3] Rosenshine, B. (2012). Principles of instruction: Research-based strategies that all teachers should know. *American Educator, 36,* 12.

practices to those being used by effective master teachers, then we'd be in trouble. How could we explain that? Happily, while learning and teaching are undeniably complex, it turns out that they are not *that* complex: we can formulate a coherent evidence-based model that links theory to practice. Rosenshine's principles provide the coherence teachers seek, and that fosters trust. This matters because without trust, teachers don't buy into information: they simply ignore it, and the inertia grows.

Authenticity

A third reason that I find is fueling interest in Rosenshine's *Principles of Instruction* is that, taken as whole, to many teachers it sounds like common sense. It's an entirely recognizable set of ideas. There are no gimmicks, no fads, nothing that seems implausible, nothing outlandish. Teachers either recognize themselves in the descriptions or they see valid and obtainable models to aspire to. After many years of having teaching defined by external powers, this feels like a grassroots document, which allows it to gain acceptance that cuts through teachers' well-honed defense systems.

From my perspective, as someone who now spends most weeks working with teachers seeking to improve their practice, it's great to have a set of ideas that are rooted so authentically in classroom experience that they are nearly uncontentious. The discussions are not about whether or not to adopt the principles; they are about how to adopt them more fluently, with more intensity, or at a higher frequency; they are about how to interpret them through the lens of each subject domain and how to adapt them for learners with different levels of knowledge and confidence.

For all these reasons, Barak Rosenshine's *Principles of Instruction* provide an incredibly useful platform for teacher development processes. It's a well-rehearsed notion that the lessons that make the difference to student outcomes are all the many lessons that go unobserved, where it is just the teacher and the students in a classroom enacting the teacher-student interactions that either lead to learning gains or don't. If teachers are going to be successful in improving their practice, they have to be working consciously and deliberately to do so. Teachers need to be working on developing better habits, seeking to be more effective day-in, day-out when nobody else except their students are looking. The kiss of death to teacher development is a school culture or accountability framework that motivates "speed camera" behaviors – where teachers turn on the style when they are under scrutiny only to revert to less effective practices the rest of the time. If we're to avoid that, then we've got to foster a professional culture where good ideas gain acceptance, credibility, and momentum. I find that in the principles we have a superb tool for doing just that.

Theory of action: What is the underlying model?

One of the big variables I find in working with teachers in a range of contexts is their ideas about how learning works. How do the actions and activities that a teacher engages in, or that they require their students to engage in, lead to learning? Sometimes teachers talk in terms of concepts "sinking in," and I often hear complaints that despite explaining a concept over and over, students still managed to misunderstand it—or even worse, despite seeming to have been successful in a lesson, they forgot it all immediately afterward. Too many teachers still believe that teaching according to students' preferred learning styles is a good idea, even though this has been soundly debunked.[4]

---

[4] Weinstein, Y., Sumeracki, M., & Caviglioli, O. (2018). *Understanding how we learn: A visual guide*. Abingdon, United Kingdom: Routledge.

All of these problems stem from a weak model of the learning process. If teachers are going to improve their practice, then it's essential for the ideas they are basing their thinking around to be formulated on a sound model. Understanding the model isn't a necessary condition for successfully implementing the strategies the model suggests, but my personal view is that teachers are more likely to connect with ideas and implement them well if they can formulate a mental model of learning that underpins the practice. This is supported by the work of Deans for Impact in their excellent "Practice with Purpose" document:

> *Deliberate practice both produces and relies on mental models and mental representations to guide decisions. These models allow practitioners to self-monitor performance to improve their performance.*[5]

It's fascinating to me just how well the *Principles of Instruction* are supported by the learning model that emerges from contemporary cognitive science. For the purposes of this short book, it will help to rehearse the key elements of this model. It is based on ideas from the following sources:

- Daniel T. Willingham's *Why Don't Students Like School* (2009)
- Graham Nuthall's *The Hidden Lives of Learners* (2007)
- Arthur Shimamura's *MARGE: A Whole-Brain Learning Approach for Students and Teachers* (2018)
- Weinstein, Sumeracki, and Caviglioli's *Understanding How We Learn* (2018)

---

[5] Deans for Impact. (2016). Practice with purpose: The emerging science of teacher expertise. Austin, TX: Deans for Impact. Retrieved from https://deans forimpact.org/wp-content/uploads/2016/12/Practice-with-Purpose_FOR -PRINT_113016.pdf

As well as the many others who collectively contribute to our current understanding, most notably Robert and Elizabeth Bjork, John Sweller, Paul Kirschener, and Carol Dweck.

A simple model for how memory works is based on the concept of building schemata in our long-term memory, as follows:

Conceptual information initially enters from the environment into our working memory.

Working memory is finite and actually rather small, so we can only absorb a limited amount of information at once.

We process information so that it is stored in our long-term memory. This is effectively unlimited, and we retrieve information back into our working memory as needed.

We organize information into schemata. Typically, new information is only stored if we can connect it to knowledge that we already have; as a result, prior knowledge is a major factor in our capacity to learn new information. The more complex and interconnected our schemata are, the easier it is to make sense of new related information and we are better able to organize it so that it makes sense. The concept of *understanding* is really "memory in disguise."[6] This means that our schemata are more fully formed, are more interconnected, and can be explored and recalled more fluently.

If a schema contains incorrect information – a misconception or an incomplete model of how a process works – we can't simply over-write it; a more primitive schema can return to dominate unless we unpick and fully re-learn a correct schema.

We forget information that we do not initially store successfully in a meaningful schema or that we do not retrieve frequently enough. This is entirely natural – we're primed to filter out information we might need and to discard the rest. Our capacity to retrieve information improves if we practice doing this more often and do so in more depth.

If we undertake enough retrieval practice, generating formulations of our memory and evaluating it for accuracy, we gain a degree of fluency and, ultimately, automaticity. This is true of anything we learn, be it reading, driving, or speaking a foreign language. A consequence of this, as explained by cognitive load theory,[7] is that the more fluent we are with retrieval of stored information, the more capacity we have in our working memory to attend to new information and problem solving. If we are efficient in bringing up the information from memory, then there's more working memory space left to deal with *applying* the information. The opposite is also true; when we are less fluent with recall, our capacity to attend to new information and problem solving is diminished. This is a key difference between novice and expert learners. Think of novice drivers,

---

[6] Willingham, D. (2009). *Why don't students like school*. San Francisco, CA: Jossey-Bass.

[7] Sweller, J., Ayres, P., & Kalyuga, S. (2011). *Cognitive load theory*. New York, NY: Springer.

who become easily overwhelmed by the pressures of traffic and road signs: they are more likely to have difficulty absorbing all the external information as well as focusing on the skill of driving itself.

A key implication of this is that novice learners need more practice than more confident, experienced learners.

Following the work of Nuthall and Shimamura, I find it instructive to imagine a classroom of students as a room full of hidden schema-forming brains, each doing things we cannot see, each processing information differently depending on what they already know, on the level of attention they are giving to the new knowledge, and on their capacity to self-regulate and to organize information successfully. In that context, instructional teaching needs to be highly interactive. We need to gain as much feedback as we can from our students, telling us how well the learning is going so that we can then plan the next steps in our teaching. Learning is hidden, so we need to seek out evidence for it in a dynamic fashion during our lessons.

This interactivity, the need for "responsive teaching,"[8] underpins many of the ideas in the *Principles of Instruction*.

Knowledge-specified curriculum

A final preliminary consideration that teachers should keep in mind before we explore the principles themselves is the notion of a knowledge-specified or "structured" curriculum. In the 1986 paper by Rosenshine and Stevens, *Teaching Functions*, they talk about the limitations of the principles:

---

[8] Wiliam, D. (2011). *Embedded formative assessment*. Bloomington, IN: Solution Tree Press.

It would be a mistake to claim that the teaching procedures which have emerged from this research apply to all subjects, and all learners, all the time. Rather, these procedures are most applicable for the "well-structured" (Simon, 1973) parts of any content area, and are least applicable to the "ill-structured" parts of any content area.

They go on to explain that all subjects have "well-structured" elements – some more than others. It's an important bit of nuance in the implementation of Rosenshine's principles. Evidently, some content needs more teacher-directed instruction than others and so the subject-specific curriculum context is important.

This also suggests that the more precise we are about the knowledge goals for learners, the more rigorous we can be about the process of ensuring that all students meet them. This rings true in my experience, having observed thousands of lessons. Very often, when engaging in feedback conversations with teachers, I feel that everyone in the class could have benefited from more precise knowledge goals – both teacher and students. It's hard to form a strong schema, to practice retrieval, or to evaluate the true extent of your knowledge if you are unsure what the knowledge is meant to be; if you are unsure what exactly "success" looks like.

This will be illustrated further as we explore each of the principles.

In the following sections, I will take each strand in turn, referencing the original seventeen instructional procedures where I think they belong. My aim is to amplify and augment the ideas as Rosenshine has expressed them, giving further examples without repeating those he used himself.

STRAND 1

Sequencing, Concepts, and Modeling

I've started here because it seems sensible to begin with elements of instruction that require advanced planning, before we get into the classroom.

Relevant instructional procedures include:

- Present new material in small steps with student practice after each step.
- Limit the amount of material students receive at one time.
- Give clear and detailed instructions and explanations.
- Think aloud and model steps.
- Use more time to provide explanations.
- Provide many examples.
- Re-teach material when necessary.

2. Present new material using small steps

Rosenshine suggests that more effective teachers recognize the need to deal with the limitations of working memory and succeed in breaking down concepts and procedures into small steps. They then ensure students have the opportunity to practice each of the steps. The modeling and scaffolding that accompany this phase of a lesson all roll into one as part of the process of explaining, providing well-structured support for students as they build their schema for new concepts.

Clearly, the implication here is that teachers need to invest time in analyzing their curriculum material to see how it can be broken down. We can't separate generic instructional methods from curriculum content in practice.

There are many examples of where material is broken down into small steps. It's a common idea in teaching sports, where complex actions and team games are built around the development of specific definable skills. In dancing, we don't try to learn a whole routine from start to finish; we learn the first step and then the second, rehearsing each one. Then we add a third and fourth and maybe practice steps one to four before adding step five. We build slowly, seeking to secure success at each point while also assimilating each part into the whole.

Many mathematical procedures are similar. Adding fractions, broken down, actually comprises several steps:

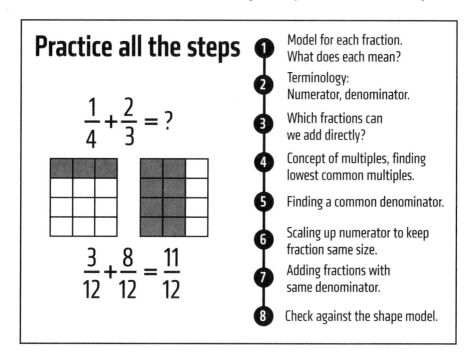

A student who struggles to add fractions may need more practice with building a concrete model of fractions as parts of shapes or may need practice finding lowest common multiples.

There are many more examples, each of which is highly subject specific. I would argue that a great deal of teacher development time would be wisely spent analyzing the curriculum, so that teachers have a clear understanding of what the learning steps might look like. Sometimes this is hard because of the *curse of knowledge* that experts experience: we don't always know what we know. We accumulate a great deal of tacit knowledge from experience in our specialist areas, and it requires some thought to map this out for our novice learners.

One common strand of thinking about new material is to break a task down into a set of instructions. How do you build a wall, and in doing so, how do you go about checking that it will be 100% straight and vertical in every plane as you go along? How do you bake a cake, from selecting and measuring the ingredients to knowing what "the right consistency" of the mixture means? How do you construct a paragraph with a particular goal in mind, selecting words and phrases to convey the meaning, create the mood, express the style that you want? How do you explain how diffusion of gases works, linking the physical reality to a model that helps explain what you see (or smell!), step by step? How do you deconstruct the process of composition in art? If teachers in the relevant discipline can break these complex activities down into fine-grained stages, they'll be more effective in explaining them to their students.

Another form of sequencing is in moving from the big picture of a subject down to a detailed area of focus and back again. We zoom out to orientate ourselves and then zoom in, ever further, step by step. This helps students to form a clear schema, locating an area of learning in relation to others. For example, each event in history has a wider context at a bigger timescale and links to a set of wider historical or social themes. Who Rosa Parks was and why what she did matters only has meaning if we know about the bigger context of the Equal Rights Movement; in biology, we go from organisms to organs to tissues to cells to cell structures and, finally, to biochemical processes. It's confusing to learn about osmosis in stomata guard cells unless we have a very clear understanding of the context of cells within a schema for plant structure and function. In poetry, in order to engage in a meaningful discussion of the specific meaning of, say, Ted Hughes' "Suddenly, he awoke and was running – raw," the opening line from "Bayonet Charge," it's going to be important to have some prior knowledge about the WWI context, and an understanding of a range of literary language techniques and structures as well as some background about Ted Hughes.

4. Provide models

Providing models is a central feature of giving good explanations. This has several meanings. Models can be:

- physical representations of completed tasks—exemplars that can be used as scaffolds, such as a model paragraph for opening a history essay
- conceptual models—such as the one we form to understand the behavior of particles in solids, liquids, and gases
- explicit narration of our thought processes when thinking through how to solve problems or undertake a creative activity

There are many ways teachers can develop their practice by developing the way they provide models:

Link abstract ideas to concrete examples

This includes the use of physical manipulatives – blocks and shapes – when learning about numbers and fractions. An important example would be equivalent fractions – using diagrams or physical objects to build a model where $\frac{1}{2} + \frac{1}{2} = \frac{1}{4} + \frac{1}{4} + \frac{3}{8} + \frac{1}{8}$. Another example is linking multiplication tables and division to a model:

$6 \times 4 = 24$. 4 rows of 6; 6 columns of 4. $24/6 = 4$.

Children are well prepared for future learning if their schema for multiplication has a secure foundation of this kind.

In English, it's helpful to know concrete examples of technical grammar structures or features of writing. "All of a sudden" is a fronted adverbial; "she glided like a swan" is a simile; "the wind swooshed and swirled around the houses" includes examples of onomatopoeia and alliteration. Moving to and fro between the abstract and the concrete is important in many aspects of language.

In science, using a molecular diagram and symbol equations to explain practical chemical reactions is essential, as with burning hydrocarbons:

Atoms are the same, but rearranged

| One methane molecule | Two oxygen molecules | One carbon dioxide molecule | Two water molecules |

$$CH_4 \quad + \quad 2O_2 \quad \rightarrow \quad CO_2 \quad + \quad 2H_2O$$

Link abstract knowledge to experiential "tacit" knowledge

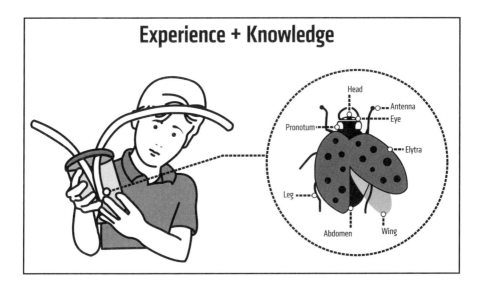

This builds directly on the section above. Concrete examples are often "tacit." As a science teacher, where the interplay of theory and practical work is well-rehearsed, I would extend Rosenshine's ideas into this important area – although it has implications in other subject domains.

In the preamble to the ten principles, Rosenshine makes an important statement following a neat summary:

> *The most effective teachers ensured that their students efficiently acquired, rehearsed, and connected background knowledge by providing a good deal of instructional support. They provided this support by teaching new material in manageable amounts, modeling, guiding student practice, helping students when they made errors, and providing for sufficient practice and review. Many of these teachers also went on to experiential, hands-on activities, but they always*

did the experiential activities after, not before, the basic material was learned.[1]

I think this needs careful interpretation in different subject contexts. Rosenshine is firmly saying that some experiential activities are not successful in securing learning unless "basic material" has been learned. Plenty of activities can seed confusion and misconceptions if students don't know enough about what they're doing. However, "tacit" knowledge can also constitute the essential background or basic material that has to be learned. In my experience, many of the phenomena taught in science can be better understood once we've gained some tacit knowledge from hands-on experience in field studies, demonstrations, or experiments. If we have studied insects by looking at them in a jar close up, then the technical work about labeling body parts and describing their form and function has a basis in our own reality. If we know what it feels like to control the speed of rotation of an electric motor, we are better placed to discuss the theoretical explanation. A well-sequenced curriculum will provide opportunities of this kind with hands-on activities in the most appropriate place to maximize learning.

Narrate the thought process

An important role for teachers is to support students in developing their capacity for metacognition and self-regulation[2] by modeling their own thought processes when engaging in a task.

[2] Rosenshine, B. (2012). Principles of instruction: Research-based strategies that all teachers should know. *American Educator, 36*, 12.

[3] Education Endowment Foundation, https://educationendowmentfoundation.org.uk/public/files/Support/Links/Campaigns/Metacognition/EEF_Metacognition_and_self-regulated_learning.pdf

Effective teachers will be able to narrate the decisions and choices they make: where to begin with a math problem; where to start with an essay; how to plan the timing of a 20-minute writing task; how to write in a style appropriate for a certain purpose and audience, making particular choices of words and phrases.

By making the implicit explicit, teachers are supporting students to form their own mental models, gaining confidence with the decisions they make.

Organize the information

Modeling can help students to organize information into secure, well-structured schema. As Shimamura suggests in the R of his MARGE[3] theory, we need to **Relate** new knowledge to what we already know. He suggests that the three C's — compare, contrast, categorize — can be helpful in doing this. Teachers can model the way complex sets of information can be sequenced, connected, and arranged into patterns to make it possible to learn and recall later.

An example of this is demonstrating how certain quotations in Shakespeare's *Macbeth* support the view of Macbeth as weak or guilt-ridden, whereas others show him to be calculating and driven by ambition. Modeling the use of quotations provides a framework for students to engage in that process themselves.

Further examples would be any context where we might categorize advantages and disadvantages or arguments for and against and, more obviously, where categories relate to physical entities: metals and nonmetals or types of tectonic plate interactions. The more teachers illustrate

---

[3] Shimamura, A. (2018). *MARGE: A whole-brain learning approach for students and teachers.* Retrieved from https://shimamurapubs.files.wordpress.com/2018/09/marge_shimamura.pdf

the formation of relational models, the more likely it is that students will grasp the ideas and form sound schemata of their own.

Worked examples *(aka worked-out examples)*

As described briefly by Rosenshine, John Sweller and others have demonstrated the power of worked examples as an outcome of cognitive load theory. Effective teachers will tend to provide students with many worked examples so that the general patterns are clear, providing a strong basis from which to learn. The trick is then to gradually reduce the level of completion, leaving students to finish problems off and ultimately do them by themselves.

Worked Examples

18% of $65	37% of $120	68% of $1050
$\dfrac{18}{100}$ x 65	$\dfrac{37}{100}$ x 120	$\dfrac{68}{100}$ x 1050
= 0.18 x 65	= 0.37 x 120	= ? x ?
= $11.70	= $44.40	=?

Rosenshine suggests that less effective teachers tend not to provide enough worked examples, thus adding to cognitive load as well as leaving students unsure of the procedures at hand and how to apply them.

Worked examples are powerful wherever calculations are involved but can also be used in any kind of structured writing or technical procedures, such as with grammar exercises in English or foreign languages, or balancing chemical equations. It's often the case that when I observe a teacher struggling to make headway with a class of students who seem stuck, I want to say, "Show them another example." So often this is the key to unlocking the next step in their understanding: seeing how it can be done.

8. Provide scaffolds for difficult tasks

Rosenshine tells us that it can be important for students to undergo a form of "cognitive apprenticeship," whereby they learn cognitive strategies from a master teacher who models, coaches, and supports them as they develop a level of independence. They key is that the scaffolds are temporary; they support the development of a cognitive process but are withdrawn so that students don't become reliant them. This is a form of guided practice as a precursor to independent practice. All of the ideas in **Principle 4. Provide Models** can be used as temporary scaffolds that are later withdrawn.

A classic example of scaffolding is the use of training wheels for learning to ride a bike. I had this experience with my own daughter. She found riding a bike difficult, so we put on training wheels that allowed her to gain confidence with steering, pedaling, and the beginnings of balance. Then, we took the training wheels off and I ran behind her holding the saddle. Eventually she called out, "You can let go now, Dad!" The beautiful thing was, I already had! She was off, riding independently. The training wheels and my saddle-holding served their purpose as she moved through the learning process.

Writing frames

In the classroom, a useful tool to scaffold writing is a writing frame. This might be the use of an opening sentence for literary analysis:

Throughout the novel, the author....	a structure that helps to discuss a long-running theme.
At first glance, the character appears......... however.....	a structure supporting comparison between surface and deep features of a character.
Both poems..... However, poem A...... whereas poem B.......	a structure for comparing two poems.

Writing frames can also be useful in science to help students organize their observations into conclusions:

Initially, the concentration is	*50% X and 50% Y*
Then, as the level of X increases	*The levels of Y decrease and the color of the mixture gets darker*
This, in turn, causes	*The flask to get warm*
So this is an	*Exothermic reaction*

A very common feature of teaching in writing-heavy subjects is to provide paragraph structures as scaffolds:

P	Point	S	Statement	P	Point
E	Evidence	Q	Quotation	E	Evidence
E	Explain	I	Inference	T	Technique
		D	Development	A	Analyze
				L	Link

The idea is to teach students how to organize their ideas. For many students, this is critical to their success in developing their knowledge of forms of expression. However, if overused, there is a risk that these paragraphs read as very formulaic, so students need to be weaned off them as they reach higher levels where a greater degree of flair and individuality is expected. The whole point of scaffolding is that, eventually, it has to be taken down!

Exemplars

A useful form of scaffolds can be the examination of exemplars produced by previous students or by the teacher. Written success criteria can feel rather dense and difficult to interpret, whereas the differences between exemplars of different standards can be much easier to understand.

If students are asked for the positive features of an exemplar and ways it can be improved, then to compare their own work to the exemplar, they can often make much better sense of the component elements that contribute to the idea of success. This can apply to writing or any creative process – an art piece or technology product.

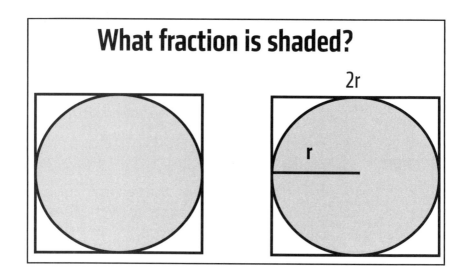

In the question above, many students who could answer the right-hand version would struggle with the left-hand version. This is simply because, in the apparent lack of any dimensions, they feel there is nothing they can do. The simple act of labeling the diagram provides a way into the problem. Once a radius is labeled, the area of the circle can be written as πr^2 and the square area can be seen to be 2r × 2r. However, students need to learn that they have the power to make the decision to undertake the labeling themselves; to introduce an algebraic variable and then use it. It's quite a big leap that needs modeling and scaffolding before students are able to do this independently with confidence.

Most problem-solving subjects have a relatively small set of archetypal problems. Once students become familiar with them, their cognitive load is greatly reduced with subsequent encounters. In this sense, simply exposing students to multiple examples of the typical problem types scaffolds their capacity for problem solving.

Anticipate errors and misconceptions

An important aspect of modeling is to anticipate common errors and to explicitly challenge misconceptions. In math and science, there are numerous well-known common misconceptions and errors; in writing, there are many common spelling and grammatical errors. A form of scaffolding is to tackle these things head-on, highlighting potential pitfalls and supporting students in checking their own work so that, ultimately, students have gained a sound knowledge of the pitfalls and are able to self-check and self-correct.

This could include basic numerical operations, such as keeping place value aligned in subtraction, multiplication, and division; or attending to the PEMDAS order of operations; checking for a positive increase when subtracting a negative number or when dividing by a number smaller than 1.

For writing, students can be provided with a checklist of common errors – periods and capital letters, correct use of apostrophes, the difference between their/there/they're – which students use initially and gradually stop relying on as they internalize the conventions.

In science, common misconceptions include the idea that the Earth's shadow causes the phases of the moon (it doesn't), that the mass of a tree comes from the soil (it comes from the air), or that "cold" can flow into a house (it's heat that flows out, reducing the temperature inside; there is no such thing as "cold" as an entity). In anticipating and teaching these ideas directly, students are able to form a more complete schema for the relevant topic.

STRAND 2 Questioning

One of the strongest implications from Rosenshine's *Principles of Instruction* is that effective questioning lies at the heart of great instructional teaching. Lined up with the work of Nuthall, Wiliam, and others, it's clear that this needs to be a highly interactive, dynamic, responsive process.

Relevant instructional procedures include:

- Ask a large number of questions and check for understanding.
- Ask students to explain what they have learned.
- Check the response of all students.
- Provide systematic feedback and corrections.

3. Ask questions

Revisiting the notion that a class is essentially a room full of highly individual, easily distracted, schema-forming brains grouped in front of us, it's vital that, as teachers, we are getting as much feedback from our students as we can. We cannot see the learning that is happening. But we can look for clues. We should be constantly wondering, *How's it going? How well have I explained this? How are they doing making sense of it?* and then solicit information to allow us to answer those questions.

A strong message from Rosenshine is that more effective teachers ask more questions, involving more students, probing in more depth, and taking more time to explain, clarify, and check for understanding. In addition, they ask students to explain the process they have used to answer a question – to narrate their thinking. Significantly, "less successful teachers ask fewer questions and almost no process questions."[1]

---

[1] Rosenshine, B. (2012). Principles of instruction: Research-based strategies that all teachers should know. *American Educator, 36,* 14.

I have found a particular repertoire of questioning strategies useful for teachers to work on, and the list below is what I usually work through in my training. In combination, these strategies unlock the full power of questioning, each seeking to achieve a particular objective. The idea is to work on one or two with deliberate practice until they form a set of organic, default modes for engaging in responsive teaching.

Cold Calling: (Based on Lemov[2], Teach Like A Champion)

Objective: If we want all students to learn all the material, then they should all be involved in engaging with the teacher-student dialogue with time to think and should not be allowed to hide, dominate, or be overlooked.

Practice: No hands up! Teachers ask questions and then select students to respond based on their knowledge of the class, avoiding the pitfalls of hands up or calling out. This is an inclusive process that conspicuously involves all students, front, back, in the corners, shy, confident . . . everyone. It's not a one-off strategy; ideally it needs to be the default mode for most questions and absolutely routine.

No Opt-Out: (Based on Lemov, 2015)

Objective: Students should feel safe in answering when unsure, but if they don't know or get things wrong, they should be given the opportunity to gain confidence by consolidating correct or secure answers. Also, students should not be allowed to form a defensive habit of saying "I don't know" simply as a get-out.

Practice: If a student or several students get an answer completely or partially wrong or they say they don't know,

---

[2] Lemov, D. (2015). *Teach like a champion 2.0: 62 techniques that put students on the path to college.* San Francisco, CA: Jossey-Bass.

move to other students or provide the correct answer. But then go back to all those students who made errors or couldn't answer, giving them a chance to now say the right answer. This gives them an opportunity for practice, but if done routinely, it also means that students soon learn there is no value in offering "I don't know" as a defense, in the hope of being left alone!

Say It Again, Better:

Objective: It's normal for first responses to be half-formed as students think aloud and formulate ideas. A second opportunity to respond allows them to finesse their answers, adding depth, accuracy, and sophistication. It's important not to inhibit students when they are unsure; it's also important not to allow them to assume mediocre answers are good enough.

Practice: When students offer a short, half-formed, or partially incorrect answer, say, "Thanks, that's great. . . . Now let's say it again better. Try again but make sure you add in X and link it to idea Y." This gives them an immediate opportunity to provide an improved response.

Think, Pair, Share:

Objective: In pairs, you can give all students space to think, to air their initial thoughts, to confess their lack of knowledge, and to prepare to give good answers (i.e., rehearse). They are all involved, and subsequent discussions then have lots of material to explore. It prevents "blood out of a stone" silences inhibiting discussion and prevents "forest of hands," with students straining to get picked or a culture of shouting out the answers, from taking hold.

Practice: Give the class a specific time-cued task – e.g., to decide on four main points in order of importance in three minutes – get them all talking in pairs and then, on time, bring them back together with a signal. Then engage in probing, cold call questioning asking them to report back what their four points were. You can also get them to explain things to each other or to take turns to quiz each other based on prompt sheets or a text.

Whole-Class Response:

Objective: Sometimes it is useful or even essential to get a response from every single student at the same time. This provides quick feedback to you as the teacher about the success of the relevant teaching and learning exchanges, identifies individuals who need further input, and can help direct subsequent questions or exercises as you respond to the feedback you gain.

Practice: My preference is for using whiteboards over any technology: they are cheap and quick and allow for responses to multiple-choice questions as well as practice sentences, calculations, diagrams – a full range. You set the question, give some response time, and then, on cue. . . . 3,2,1 Show Me. . . . Students all show their answers at once. A simple *A, B, C, D = 1,2,3,4* show of fingers also works very well for multiple-choice. It's vital to engage with the responses. and then to adjust your teaching accordingly, consolidating, re-explaining, or moving on as appropriate.

In situations where new vocabulary is being introduced, teachers can get good results from using tightly orchestrated choral repetition: here, all students are involved, gaining confidence from the practice under cover of the class' collective voice.

Probing:

Objective: In order to explore a student's schema in any depth, teachers need to ask the student several questions. Only asking a series of single questions in turn to several students provides shallow responses compared to when each student has provided multiple responses. Probing each student's schema with multiple responsive questions is a powerful mode of questioning and a form of guided practice.

Practice: Make it the default that, in any given exchange, you are asking each student, 3,4,5 questions before moving on, probing for understanding, checking for misconceptions, adding extra challenge, and providing scaffolding to engineer success. Rosenshine provides some good examples of this in his principles. Here's my view of what a teacher might be saying in dialogue with students:

- That's interesting, what makes you say that?
  - That's true, but why do you think that is?
- Is there a different way to say the same thing?
  - Can you give an example of where that happens?
- Can you explain how you worked that out?
  - So, what happens if we made it bigger or smaller?
- Why? Are you sure? Is there another explanation?
  - Which of those things makes the biggest impact?
- What is the theme that links all those ideas together?
  - What is the evidence that supports that suggestion?
- Does anyone agree with that? Why?
  - Does anyone disagree? What would you say instead? Why is that different?
- How does that answer compare to that answer?
  - But what's the reason for that? And how is that connected to the first part?

- How did you know that? What made you think of that? Where did that idea come from?
  - Is that always true or just in this example?
- What would be the opposite of that?
  - Is it true for everyone or just some people?
- Is that a direct cause of the effect or is it just a coincidence, a correlation?

6. Check for student understanding

In his 1982 paper, standing out in the whole list of teaching functions, Rosenshine underlines _Checks for Understanding_, adopting the acronym CFU. This appears to be at the center of the whole process – something I'd whole-heartedly support from my experience observing and teaching hundreds of lessons. For me, it's the core concept in the principles. Based on my recent work as a teacher trainer, I'd suggest that CFU is probably the single biggest common area for improvement in the teaching that I see, so I'm happy to see Rosenshine literally underlining it as being important. (Unsurprisingly, it's also a prominent theme in Doug Lemov's _Teach Like a Champion_.[3])

Here is a superb excerpt from Teaching Functions where Rosenshine (1986) explains how **not** to do CFU:

> The wrong way to check for understanding is to ask
> only a few questions, call on volunteers to hear their
> (usually correct) answers, and then assume that all
> of the class either understands or has now learned
> from hearing the volunteers' responses. Another
> error is to ask, "are there any questions?" and, if there

---

[3] Lemov, D. (2015). *Teach like a champion 2.0: 62 techniques that put students on the path to college.* San Francisco, CA: Jossey-Bass.

aren't any, assume that everybody understands.
Another error (particularly with older children)
is to assume that it is not necessary to check for
understanding, and that simply repeating the points
will be sufficient.[4]

I love this. It's all too common. A scenario I often use to highlight this problem is to ask people to imagine the process of teaching something with high-stakes outcomes like rappelling (abseiling). If your goal is for your team of novice rappelers to rappel independently – safely reaching the ground – you would go a lot further than simply demonstrating the technique and asking, "Are there any questions?" or assuming one student's correct modeling of the procedure indicated the likely success of the others. You would definitely check that everyone could do it and give them all plenty of practice.

And yet, in lessons, teachers use these rhetorical, self-report questions and crude assumptions of understanding all the time – with adding fractions or conjugating verbs! It's high risk, in learning terms.

If we are going to be sure all students have formed secure understanding, teachers should not assume that knowledge aired and shared in the public space of the classroom has been absorbed and learned by any individual. It's necessary to check for understanding from students to determine whether they understood what you meant. Do they now have the level of understanding you are aiming at?

An example might be similar to the question I often use in my training: Why does the Sun rise in the east? People often think they know this – until they start to explain it to someone else!

---

[4] Page 388 from Rosenshine, B., & Stevens, R. J. (1986). Teaching functions. In M. C. Wittrock (Ed.), *Handbook of research on teaching* (pp. 376–391, 3rd ed.). New York, NY: Macmillan.

Why does the Sun rise in the east?

The process we undertake in answering a question like this is to generate a new version of what we've previously learned; we then evaluate that version to determine if it is complete and correct. A silent self-checking process is powerful in itself, but we might also get the class to explain to each other in pairs; this helps to engage everyone. The teacher can then sample the class to check the understanding of individuals. Importantly, the teacher should be asking the student to run through their whole explanation to determine the accuracy of the student's schema, not just a small part of it.

After any exposition or question exchange with a particular student, the process suggested by *Principles of Instruction* is that teachers should ask a number of other students to relay back what they have understood. Always, instead of "Do you understand?" you should ask "Can you tell me what you have understood?" It's a radically different question.

Even if they are answering a question that someone else has already answered, it's valuable for other students to be given a chance to offer their version, showing what they have understood and, in so doing, giving the teacher feedback about how successful the teaching has been. It's especially powerful to ask multiple students, often yielding various different responses which throw up subtle points for further teaching. This can be combined with all-student response questioning with mini whiteboards or other short writing tasks where everyone generates a response to show their understanding as the teacher circulates the class.

There are two key benefits from regularly checking for understanding:

a) The teacher gains feedback about which part of the material might need to be revisited, re-taught, or given more practice time.

b) In rehearsing their understanding, students are likely to be elaborating on the knowledge in the relevant schemata, which will strengthen connections between different ideas and improve long-term retention. The checking helps them remember more the next time they check.

Rosenshine suggests that the importance of checking for understanding reinforces the need to present material in small steps. If we allow students to try to construct a mental summary of too much material at once, they can introduce errors that then become stored in their schema as a learned misconception. This is especially true where students' prior background knowledge is weak for a given concept. If we check for understanding with smaller amounts of material, we're likely to be supporting students in forming stronger, more reliable schemata.

Checking for understanding can work at a general overview level to support teacher instruction, but it can become quite forensic when we are focusing on maximizing individual success. For example a teacher might construct a definitive answer following a class discussion or predetermine what a good answer should contain. They can then use this as a focus for their CFU process as students write individual answers or explain verbally:

Why does the Sun rise in the east?	Success?
Before sunrise, the **Sun is at a distance**, not visible to the part of the Earth experiencing night.	
Earth rotates → anticlockwise (looking from North Pole)	
As night moves to day, the Sun appears on **east horizon**, to our left if we stand facing south.	
The **impression of "rising" is an illusion**; it is the Earth rotating relative to the Earth-Sun line.	

In general, I would advocate placing Checking for Understanding right at the center of teachers' thinking during their lessons. It forces us to consider the detail of what we want all students to know and how, exactly, to organize the lesson to maximize the number and the depth of student responses we can engage with.

Reviewing Material

A major issue in learning is the inevitable, predictable, and natural process of forgetting. Unless we review what we've learned, our memory of that information diminishes; we remember fewer details and fewer connections and find it harder to retrieve what we previously learned. Retrieval practice supports building our long-term memory and our level of fluency in recall.

Relevant instructional procedures from Rosenshine include:

- Begin a lesson with a short review of previous learning.
- Re-teach material when necessary.

1. Daily Review

One of the purposes of daily review is to support the development of fluency, as explored below, with weekly and monthly review. The significance of daily review is that it allows students to re-activate recently acquired knowledge, reducing cognitive load at the beginning of a lesson that's designed to build on this knowledge. Students don't necessarily recall recent learning readily, and it pays to anticipate this rather than be frustrated by it. It's also important for prior learning to be active in our working memory if we're going to add more layers of complexity to it; the connections we want to engineer won't happen otherwise.

A very common example might be the use of new terminology or vocabulary. It might be that yesterday we learned the new word: *sesquipedalian*: *tending to use long words; long-winded*. Today, we want to use knowledge of that word to explore a text. We could start the lesson with a multiple-choice question which everyone is required to answer independently, justifying their choice of correct response and all the incorrect responses:

Which sentence uses the word *sesquipedalian* most appropriately?

a) Sesquipedalian people are in their 70s.
b) The man felt sesquipedalian after his operation.
c) John was a rather sesquipedalian speaker; his audiences would sometime lose focus.
d) The speech was full of sesquipedalian facts that didn't support her main argument.

It's not just a case of saying, "Does everyone remember what we learned yesterday?" The question makes the students explore their understanding.

Another example might be the use of a quotation from a literacy text:

Based on yesterday's lesson, complete the quotation and then, in a pair, discuss the significance of this quotation from Act 3: Scene 2 in *Macbeth*.

O, full of _____ *is* _____, _____. *(Oh, full of scorpions is my mind, dear wife.)*

We might also ask students for some straightforward factual recall.

- We learned five key advantages of wind power over coal-fired power – what were they?
- We practiced some angle facts questions yesterday try the three questions on the slide to refresh your memory – the first one is partially completed to get you started.

As cognitive scientist Efrat Furst (2019) explains in her work[1] on understanding "understanding" and reconsolidation of memory, there is a natural time delay factor that teachers should take into account in their teaching. It's entirely natural for students to experience some short-term confusion and lack of fluency as they encounter new material because we don't re-wire our brains instantaneously. A daily review routine can serve the purpose of checking in to see that, with some time having passed, students have secured the knowledge required in their memory in good enough shape to go build on it further.

---

[1] Furst, E. (2019). Understanding understanding [Blog post]. Retrieved from https://sites.google.com/view/efratfurst/understanding-understanding

10. Weekly and Monthly Review

One main purpose of weekly and monthly review is to ensure that previously learned material is not forgotten – to attenuate the natural rate of forgetting. It is also to ensure that, through frequent revisiting of a range of material, students are able to form ever more well-connected networks of ideas – more extensive schemata. This form of practice helps students to learn more information and makes it easier to be successful with problem solving as less space in short-term memory is needed.

More effective teachers routinely engage students in a variety of forms of retrieval practice, recalling and applying previously learned material.

In this example, suppose that we want all students to know some key events in the Civil Rights story, including the dates. A task might be to get them to study the timeline notes on the left and then, the following week, to get them to complete the blank dates for the shuffled set of events on the right. This is something they can practice at home and can check for themselves. Where possible, if students can check their own answers, so much the better. A week later, we might give them a table of dates and ask students to fill in the events, to mix up the way in which the material is being test.

1955	Montgomery Bus Boycott
1960	Freedom Summer
1963	March on Washington
1964	Civil Rights Act
1965	Rise of Black Power
1968	MLK Assassinated

?	Civil Rights Act
?	Freedom Summer
?	March on Washington
?	MLK Assassinated
?	Montgomery Bus Boycott
?	Rise of Black Power

Of course, knowing the dates is only the baseline for more advanced pieces of work. The idea is that, where students have more fluent recall of these basic facts, they have more space in working memory to attend to applying the knowledge to explain deeper questions.

Another form of retrieval practice is utilizing the memory-building power of narrative structures. It's not all about simple recall tests! One example could be to review understanding and recall of the water cycle. Students are asked to tell the story of a water molecule, starting in the sea, using the correct terminology for changes of state and using the concept of energy.

Students then, individually or in pairs, engage in elaborative-interrogative questioning. How does this happen? Why did that happen? This type of questioning has been shown to have a strong effect on future retention[2] as it forces us to form more coherent schemata.

Finally, it's important to remember that we are all prey to the illusion of familiarity. As Shimamura explains in the G and E of MARGE[3] – **Generate/Evaluate** – we can easily think we've learned something if the information is continually presented to us. We see ideas laid out that we recognize, so we tell ourselves that we've learned them. However, in order to evaluate our recall and understanding,

[2] Weinstein, Y., Sumeracki, M., & Caviglioli, O. (2018). *Understanding how we learn: A visual guide.* Abingdon, United Kingdom: Routledge.
[3] Shimamura, A. (2018). *MARGE: A whole-brain learning approach for students and teachers.* Retrieved from https://shimamurapubs.files .wordpress.com/2018/09/marge_shimamura.pdf

we must generate versions of that information from memory without looking at the source. This tells us, as the learner, what we know and don't know – even before our teacher gets to find out.

An example I've explored for myself is the process of learning key facts and narratives about the famous story of King Henry VIII's six wives. Having read about them several times, I nonetheless found myself forgetting key details. So, in order to strengthen my recall, I re-studied the material focusing on more specific information – names, marriage dates, their fate – and then generated this timeline from memory. I evaluated the information I generated from memory by checking with the source, adding and correcting details, and repeating the process several days later. It worked!

Henry VIII's Six Wives

Anne of Cleves
Married 1540
Divorced 1540

Catherine Howard
Married 1540
Beheaded 1542

Catherine d'Aragon
Married 1509
Divorced 1533

1500   1530   1540   1550

Henry born 1491

Henry VII dies
Henry VIII becomes King in 1509

Anne Boleyn
Married 1533
Beheaded 1536

Catherine Parr
Married 1543
Died 1548

Mary
Born 1516
⊕ C of A

Elizabeth
Born
⊕33

Jane Seymour
Married 1536
Died 1537

Henry
Died 1547

Edward
Born 1537
⊕ JS

I found that it helped me to recall the information as I added more layers of narrative around each of the women. Once Anne Boleyn or Catherine Howard have distinctive characters and life stories, they cease to be bland names on a page; the schema I have for them are more complete and I have more connections to other schemata, the basis for fluency.

More generally, the idea that learning is a *generative process* is important. Daily, weekly, and monthly review activities give students opportunities to generate versions of what they know and understand, helping to strengthen future retrieval of the knowledge involved, build fluency, and identify where they might have residual gaps or areas of uncertainty.

In summary, to make daily, weekly, and monthly review part of an effective and sustainable routine, I suggest that the following principles should apply:

- Involve everyone: Good techniques involve all students checking their knowledge, not just a few and not just one at a time as you might do when questioning.
- Make checking accurate and easy: It should be possible for all students to find out what they got right and wrong, what they know well, and where they have gaps. Good techniques involve students testing their knowledge and then checking their work for accuracy and completeness. This is not the same as giving students extended rubrics to grade longer assessments beyond a simple retrieval practice activity.
- Specify the knowledge: Where appropriate, it's better if students know the set of knowledge any retrieval will be based on, so they can study, prepare, and self-check. It must be possible for students to check their own answers.
- Keep it generative: Students need to explore their memory to check what they know and understand; this means removing cue cards, prompts, scaffolds, and cheat sheets. It means closing the books and making students think for themselves.
- Vary the diet: Mix up the use of teacher-led, self-quizzing, written and verbal quizzing, self-explanation,

"telling the story," multiple-choice and open-response tests, rehearsing explanations, summarizing, creating knowledge maps, demonstration and performance of learned techniques, routines, and procedures. This will allow students to explore their schemata in different ways, strengthening future recall.

- Make it time efficient: A good technique can be used repeatedly in an efficient manner without dominating whole lessons.
- Make it workload efficient: The best methods do not involve the teacher checking the students' answers, creating an unsustainable workload. A teacher might choose to check the occasional test, but for routine practice, students should do it themselves.

One of the reasons I am such a big fan of Rosenshine's *Principles of Instruction* is that it brings the idea of practice to the fore. As a profession, we have been through a period where ideas such as rote learning, repetition, or drill have been disparaged and scoffed at as old-fashioned—even characterized as being against the spirit of great learning. Once you de-demonize these ideas, reconstituting them simply as *practice*, they seem entirely sensible as part of a sound learning process. Nobody ever excels at anything without lots of practice, and that starts with the way we conduct our lessons.

Relevant instructional procedures include:

- Provide a high level of practice for all students.
- Guide students as they begin to practice.
- Prepare students for independent practice.
- Monitor students when they begin independent practice.

The distinction between guided practice and independent practice is a hallmark of Rosenshine's thinking.

5. Guide student practice

Rosenshine suggests that, in the observational research, the most effective teachers gave more time for guided practice, which is directly linked to them spending more time asking questions and more time checking for understanding and using more worked examples. The idea is that, if students are going to be successful in becoming confident and independent within a certain knowledge area, the teacher needs to make sure they are forming a strong schema early on.

Importantly, we actually need a broad view of what might constitute practice. In this section of *Principles*, Rosenshine says:

> *An important finding from information-processing research is that students need to spend additional time rephrasing, elaborating, and summarizing new material in order to store this material in their long-term memory.*

This gives us a steer as to the kinds of cognitive processes students might engage in when practicing. There are many ways to revisit material so that the schema-forming process is successful.

All students need to practice – but that practice must be guided so that the chance of forming misconceptions is minimized. Not only that, the guidance is key to generating the high success rate that in turn fuels motivation and engagement during more independent work. The less confident learners are, and the less prior knowledge they have, then the more important guided practice is. As students gain in knowledge and confidence, the guided practice phase can become shorter or can cover large amounts of material at once.

In essence, guided practice is typically where learning activities involve thorough explanations; high-frequency, short-answer questions; or simple tasks where the teacher and students are engaged interactively, with plenty of modeling, corrective or affirming feedback, and aspects of re-teaching where gaps remain. If students are involved in what Rosenshine calls *seatwork*, then the teacher would be circulating, looking closely at student responses to check for early errors or successes. With insufficient early practice or guidance, students often flounder with subsequent independent tasks.

Guided practice can be applied to learning in so many ways, building fluency and ultimately developing a level of automaticity with recall. To a great extent, asking questions and checking for understanding (Strand 2) are forms of guided practice. The ideas explored for modeling and scaffolding (Strand 1) are all part of guided practice. It's here that the *Principles of Instruction* strongly overlap and reinforce each other.

One of the issues teachers sometimes have is in generating a high level of repetition that involves all students. As well as the more obvious method of setting exercises with multiple questions of the same type, I have seen teachers make excellent use of choral repetition and quick-fire questioning to achieve high-frequency repetition. These strategies can be used in any lesson, including the following:

Fronted adverbials for dramatic impact: Students practice these sentences, repeatedly stating the stem with each variation that they made up.

Quick as a flash..... *he disappeared behind the fence; he climbed the tower; she conjured up a potion.*

All of a sudden...... s*he fell down a hole; giant hailstones began to fall; he changed his mood.*

Students are less likely to use phrases independently if they have not had a chance to practice them first.

Number bonds to 100: The teacher calls out a number 0-100 and the students chant back the bond to hundred, which is easily then extended to 1000 or any other number.

56..... 44!!

87......13!!

23......77!!

The objective is to increase fluency through the speed of response. The more often they do it, the better they get.

Foreign language: In a French lesson, students learn a new phrase and how to say it with a good accent by using it repeatedly. The guided practice phase involves whole-class choral repetition with the teacher first modeling the French, but then switching to give only the English.

Où que j'aille / Où que j'aille / Où que j'aille (Wherever I go)

quoi que je fasse / quoi que je fasse / quoi que je fasse (whatever I do)

Où que j'aille, quoi que je fasse : Où que j'aille, quoi que je fasse / Où que j'aille, quoi que je fasse

Wherever I go: Où que j'aille

Whatever I do: quoi que je fasse

Wherever I go, whatever I do: Où que j'aille, quoi que je fasse.

Wherever I go, whatever I do, the sun always shines: Où que j'aille, quoi que je fasse, le soleil brille toujours.

Wherever I go, whatever I do, I always find litter: Où que j'aille, quoi que je fasse, je trouve toujours des déchets.

The choral work is often punctuated with selecting individuals to respond, picking up on details of syntax and pronunciation. The confidence building that comes from these activities is significant.

A common feature of practice is repetition. Sometimes practice activities are unsuccessful because students are practicing too many things at one time and, therefore, they are not practicing any one thing often enough. This can be true in language lessons where too many new words and grammar features are being practiced; it can be true of extended writing tasks where students are wrestling with the content, structure, language, grammar – and flounder under the weight of it all. The trick is to break down tasks, as suggested by Principle 2 (Strand 1), so that repeated practice of smaller steps can be achieved before they are assimilated into more complex tasks.

7. Obtain a high success rate

The research Rosenshine refers to includes studies that show that more effective teachers set questions and tasks with sufficient practice to engineer a high success rate – with an optimal level around 80% success. He even suggests that going down to 70% is too low. If students are getting too much wrong, then they are effectively practicing making errors! This can then form part of what is learned and be hard to overcome.

The idea is that at 80% most of what students are doing is reinforcing error-free, secure learning, improving fluency and confidence. This then provides a stronger platform for subsequent learning. However, we are not talking about 90-95% in the early stages. It's important that students are challenged and that they have learning goals that are ahead of them. It's a well-established aspect of growth mindset research[1] that, in order to succeed, students need to approach challenges with a positive attitude, with the confidence to learn from mistakes and not to be

[1] E.g., Yeager, D., Walton, G., & Cohen, G. L. (2013). Addressing achievement gaps with psychological interventions. *Phi Delta Kappan, 94*(5), 62–65. Retrieved from https://labs.la.utexas.edu/adrg/files/2013/12/PDK-Yeager -Walton-Cohen-2013.pdf

afraid of making them. This is how we reach high levels of achievement: we stretch beyond our current capabilities, working hard at a strategy until it yields success, or changing strategy to find a better path. We then practice that successful strategy to increase fluency and push on again. It's as much about strategy as it is about effort.

The implication for teachers is that we need to continually evaluate the success rate of our students:

> *If their success rate is too low – we may need to go back: to re-teach, re-explain, re-model; to return to more secure ground and build back up again, perhaps trying different approaches. We then need to give students more guided practice at a strategy that allows them to reach the nominal 80% threshold. Nothing new, just more practice.*

> *If their success is much higher than 80%, it suggests they are ready for more challenge. We need to add levels of depth in the knowledge requirements in the task, to set more difficult problems, to require deeper explanations, to remove some of the scaffolds and supports.*

In my view, it's unrealistic to achieve this neatly for all students in a mixed-attainment class, minute by minute. The 80% goal is more appropriate as an overarching benchmark over the course of a series of lessons – supporting more here, challenging more there, nudging, stretching, pushing, giving clues, adding support, taking support away... It's a combination of the minutiae of classroom interactions with planning of tasks and resources that allows for success at different rates or degrees of depth depending on where students are in their learning. Also, as we reach the conclusion of a topic, you might well expect students to be getting closer to 100% right on a knowledge test: that would be the explicit goal.

9. Independent practice

In many ways, this is the ultimate goal for teaching: to construct learning so that students are able to do challenging things by themselves without help. *"The more successful teachers provided for extensive and successful practice, both in the classroom and after class."*[2] Less effective teachers may not only cut guided practice short; they also do not provide enough opportunity for independent practice. Judging the transition from students needing strong guidance to becoming independent learners is a subtle skill; it's a central element of teacher expertise that develops with knowing the material, knowing how to break it down into practicable elements, and crucially, knowing the students.

Rosenshine suggests that it is important for the material students practice to be the same during independent practice as during guided practice in order for the appropriate level of success to be secured. During independent practice, success rates need to be as high as possible – especially if the teacher is not present to provide corrective feedback.

---

[2] Rosenshine, B. (2012). Principles of instruction: Research-based strategies that all teachers should know. *American Educator, 36*, 19.

The basic flow of many learning experiences is this:

	Strand 1: Sequencing Concepts and Modeling	Strand 2: Questioning	Strand 4: Stages of Practice	Strand 3: Reviewing Material
Teacher explains.				
Teacher models.				
Student engages in guided practice with scaffolding as needed.				
Teacher checks for understanding.				
Scaffolding and support are gradually withdrawn.				
Student engages in independent practice.				
Student becomes fluent.				

A simpler version that I like is: I do it; we do it; you do it: I. We. You. However we express it, it is vital that students are given ample opportunities to perform tasks by themselves. This applies whether they are using new vocabulary in speech or writing, performing mathematical operations, explaining any kind of natural phenomenon, telling a story, making an argument, playing a piece of music, or performing a piece of theatre.

I've seen a great example of this not working well. A kindergarten teacher was trying to broaden her students' vocabulary, working around a well-known witches story. On the board, there were various words and suggestions captured during class discussion. The teacher was aiming at something like: *The wicked witch had gnarled fingers and terrible twisted toes.*

We came into the class as visitors and the teacher selected a student to showcase their work.

> Teacher: Janine, tell the visitors what we know
> about the witch?
> Janine: *The witch was really bad.*

The teacher was crestfallen, but the problem was obvious. Janine had not had nearly enough independent practice using the target words to gain a level of confidence and fluency. Under pressure to perform she reverted to her confidence base – her more basic vocabulary. I see this kind of thing all the time.

I've seen many excellent examples, including the use of well-structured collaborative learning – or *cooperative learning* as Rosenshine calls it. One example I observed was students practicing how to explain how a transformer works after a guided practice phase involving teacher questioning. The transformer has about six major steps running from an input voltage to an output voltage via an iron core and various coils and magnetic fields. One student in each pair had their knowledge organizer that detailed each step alongside a labeled diagram; the partner student had a blank diagram. Without notes, the task was to rehearse the full explanation in detail, giving the student an opportunity to practice generating, elaborating, and communicating the details of their mental model of the process; the partner served as a verifier. They then swapped and later applied the same process to other electromagnetic devices. It was a highly effective, energetic lesson.

Other simple examples include French lessons where students engage in dialogues based on their recent learning without using their notes; math lessons where students simply attempt extensive problem sets building on their recent learning; and English lessons where students write paragraphs or essays without structured supports, consolidating the knowledge content and techniques they have just acquired.

An essential feature of independent practice is that students draw on their own resources. This is where they have to rely on recall from memory, building fluency through repeatedly engaging in processes that reinforce connections and retrieval pathways, generating their own feedback, and setting their own goals for improvement. The teacher's role is to provide students with the tools they need to do this, including teaching them explicit strategies for checking their own work against a set of standards in a form they can understand, using exemplars or success criteria.

To Wrap It Up...

As a teacher and teacher-trainer, I have found that Barak Rosenshine's *Principles of Instruction* provide a superb structure for supporting the process of professional development. All the principles overlap – as is evident reading the "Principles" paper; several key ideas around practice and the ways cognitive processes link to classroom activities are repeated in each section. However, it is useful to consider each strand one by one:

1) Sequencing Concepts and Modeling
2) Questioning
3) Reviewing Material
4) Stages of Practice

In each case, the question we should ask is not "Do we do this?" Most teachers will say that they do. We all ask questions; we all get students to practice; we all try to sequence concepts in small steps. The question we should ask is "How well do we do this?" For me, this is where the power of *Principles of Instruction* lies, because we can all get better at delivering on each strand.

- We can all find better ways to sequence concepts with more effective models and forms of scaffolding.
- We can all increase the intensity of questioning and the depth of checking for understanding, increasing the ratio of students involved.
- We can all improve our efficiency and success with reviewing material, securing better levels of retention and more sophisticated responses.
- We can all develop ever-better ways of engineering high success rates as we move skillfully from guided to independent practice.

Importantly, it is unrealistic and unhelpful to work on each of these improvement agendas simultaneously. Teachers and their leaders should use *Principles of Instruction* as a source of guidance and as a self-reflection tool, but it is essential for long-term success to improve one thing at time.

It's also important to recognize that most subjects require a diet of activities and lesson types that vary over time, and it would not be reasonable or sensible to expect to see each of these principles being modeled during any given one-off lesson observation.

Please, please, please do not corrupt the spirit and intent of *Principles of Instruction* by turning it into a lesson-by-lesson checklist. Use it to lift people up, not to tie them down!

Finally, it's essential that we develop subject-specific models around it. We already suffer enough genericism in education, and it would be a mistake to impose *a Principles of Instruction* formula of some kind into areas where it does not belong. For each subject domain, teachers should consider how the principles or the four strands apply.

There is always knowledge; there is always practice; there is always a role for checking for understanding – but the way these things take form varies significantly from Physics to Spanish to History to Art to Drama to Math and to Science. Let's celebrate that variety and not seek to confine it.

Thank you to Barak Rosenshine for the gift you've given us in *Principles of Instruction*. I have already met many hundreds of teachers who have found it immensely supportive in making their day-to-day work in the classroom more rewarding and more productive as they seek to lead their students to excellence, and I know for sure there will thousands more to follow in the future.

Works Cited and Further Reading

Deans for Impact. (2016). Practice with purpose: The emerging science of teacher expertise. Austin, TX: Deans for Impact. Retrieved from https://deansforimpact.org/wp-content/uploads/2016/12/Practice-with-Purpose_FOR-PRINT_113016.pdf

Furst, E. (2019). Understanding understanding [Blog post]. Retrieved from https://sites.google.com/view/efratfurst/understanding-understanding

Hattie, J. (2009). *Visible learning: A synthesis of over 800 meta-analyses relating to achievement.* Abingdon, United Kingdom: Routledge.

Lemov, D. (2015). *Teach like a champion 2.0: 62 techniques that put students on the path to college.* San Francisco, CA: Jossey-Bass.

Nuthall, G. (2007). *The hidden lives of learners.* Wellington, New Zealand: NZCER Press.

Quigley, A., Muijs, D., & Stringer, E. (2018). *Metacognition and self-regulated learning guidance report*. London, United Kingdom: Education Endowment Foundation.

Rosenshine, B. (1982). *Teaching Functions in Instructional Programmes*. Washington, DC: National Institute of Education.

Rosenshine, B. (2010). *Principles of instruction*. Educational Practices Series 21. Brussels, Belgium: The International Academy of Education. Retrieved from http://www.ibe.unesco.org/fileadmin/user_upload/Publications/Educational_Practices/EdPractices_21.pdf

Rosenshine, B. (2012). Principles of instruction: Research-based strategies that all teachers should know. *American Educator, 36*, 12–19, 39.

Rosenshine, B., & Stevens, R. J. (1986). Teaching functions. In M. C. Wittrock (Ed.), *Handbook of research on teaching* (pp. 376–391, 3rd ed.). New York, NY: Macmillan.

Shimamura, A. (2018). *MARGE: A whole-brain learning approach for students and teachers*. Retrieved from https://shimamurapubs.files.wordpress.com/2018/09/marge_shimamura.pdf

Sweller, J., Ayres, P., & Kalyuga, S. (2011). *Cognitive load theory*. New York, NY: Springer.

Weinstein, Y., Sumeracki, M., & Caviglioli, O. (2018). *Understanding how we learn: A visual guide*. Abingdon, United Kingdom: Routledge.

Wiliam, D. (2011). *Embedded formative assessment*. Bloomington, IN: Solution Tree Press.

Willingham, D. (2009). *Why don't students like school*. San Francisco, CA: Jossey-Bass.

Yeager, D., Walton, G., & Cohen, G. L. (2013). Addressing achievement gaps with psychological interventions. *Phi Delta Kappan, 94*(5), 62–65. Retrieved from https://labs.la.utexas.edu/adrg/files/2013/12/PDK-Yeager-Walton-Cohen-2013.pdf